Teresa

by Lola M. Schaefer

Consulting Editor: Gail Saunders-Smith, Ph.D.

Consultant: Merlyn Mowrey, Associate Professor,
Department of Philosophy and Religion,
Central Michigan University

Pebble Books

an imprint of Capstone Press
Mankato, Minnesota

Pebble Books are published by Capstone Press
151 Good Counsel Drive, P.O. Box 669, Mankato, Minnesota 56002
www.capstonepub.com

Library of Congress Cataloging-in-Publication Data
Schaefer, Lola M., 1950–
     Mother Teresa / by Lola M. Schaefer.
     p. cm.—(First biographies)
     Summary: Simple text and photographs introduce the life of Mother
Teresa, who founded an order of nuns called the Missionaries of Charity
to take care of the poor in India.
     Includes bibliographical references and index.
     ISBN 13: 978-0-7368-1646-5 (hardcover)
     ISBN 10: 0-7368-1646-1 (hardcover)
     ISBN 13: 978-0-7368-3381-3 (paperback)
     ISBN 10: 0-7368-3381-1 (paperback)
     1. Teresa, Mother, 1910– —Juvenile literature. 2. Missionaries of Charity—
Biography—Juvenile literature. [1. Teresa, Mother, 1910– 2. Missionaries of Charity.
3. Missionaries. 4. Nuns. 5. Nobel Prizes—Biography. 6. Women—Biography.]
I. Title. II. Series: First biographies (Mankato, Minn.)
BX4406.5.Z8 S33 2003
271'.97—dc21   2002011744

Note to Parents and Teachers

The First Biographies series supports national history standards for units on people and culture. This book describes and illustrates the life of Mother Teresa. The photographs support early readers in understanding the text. This book also introduces early readers to subject-specific vocabulary words, which are defined in the Words to Know section. Early readers may need assistance to read some words and to use the Table of Contents, Words to Know, Read More, Internet Sites, and Index/Word List sections of the book.

Printed in the United States of America in North Mankato, Minnesota
072011   006231CGVMI

Table of Contents

Time Line

1910
born

Agnes Bojaxhiu was born in 1910 in what is now Macedonia. Her parents were Albanian. Her mother taught her to be kind to people who are sick or poor.

◄ the Macedonian countryside

Time Line

1910
born

Agnes went to a Catholic church and a Catholic school. She prayed at church. She sang in the choir. She read about missionary work.

modern-day Catholics praying in church

Time Line

1910
born

1922
receives call to
help others

At age 12, Agnes had
a calling. She believed
God wanted her to help
others. Agnes decided
to become a nun.

Agnes (left) and her sister as young women

Time Line

1910
born

1922
receives call to
help others

1937
becomes
a nun

Agnes studied at three convents. She changed her name to Sister Teresa. In 1937, she became a nun.

students at a convent where Agnes studied

Time Line

1910
born

1922
receives call to
help others

1937
becomes
a nun

12

For many years, Sister Teresa lived in a convent in India. She worked as a teacher. Then she decided to study nursing.

Time Line

1910	1922	1937
born	receives call to help others	becomes a nun

14

Sister Teresa cared for people who were sick and dying. She gave food, shelter, and kindness to poor people in India.

poor people in India

Time Line

1910
born

1922
receives call to
help others

1937
becomes
a nun

Many nuns wanted to help Sister Teresa. In 1950, she became the leader of a new group of nuns called the Missionaries of Charity. Her name became Mother Teresa.

 Missionaries of Charity nuns at prayer

1950
forms new
group of nuns

Time Line

1910
born

1922
receives call to
help others

1937
becomes
a nun

Mother Teresa and her nuns opened schools for poor people. They took care of unwanted babies and children without families.

1950
forms new
group of nuns

Time Line

●	●	●
1910	1922	1937
born	receives call to help others	becomes a nun

20

Mother Teresa won the Nobel Peace Prize in 1979. She died in 1997. Mother Teresa lived to serve God and the poor.

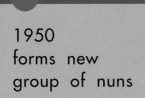

1950
forms new
group of nuns

1979
wins Nobel
Peace Prize

1997
dies

Words to Know

calling—a strong urge or desire to do something

Catholic Church—one particular Christian church with its own beliefs and rules

choir—a group of people who sing together

convent—a building where Catholic nuns live and work together

missionary—someone who is sent by a church or religious group to teach that group's faith and do good works

Nobel Peace Prize—an award given to a person who helps bring about peace in the world

nun—a Catholic woman who lives in a religious community and has promised to devote her life to God

Read More

Ransom, Candice F. *Mother Teresa*. On My Own Biography. Minneapolis: Carolrhoda Books, 2001.

Ross, Stewart. *The Story of Mother Teresa*. Lifetimes. North Mankato, Minn.: Thameside Press, 2001.

Wheeler, Jill C. *Mother Teresa*. Breaking Barriers. Minneapolis: Abdo Publications, 2002.

Internet Sites

Track down many sites about Mother Teresa. Visit the FACT HOUND at *http://www.facthound.com*

IT IS EASY! IT IS FUN!

1) Go to *http://www.facthound.com*

2) Type in: 0736816461

3) Click on "FETCH IT" and FACT HOUND will find several links hand-picked by our editors.

Relax and let our pal FACT HOUND do the research for you!

Index/Word List

Word Count: 206
Early-Intervention Level: 17

Editorial Credits
Jennifer VanVoorst, editor; Heather Kindseth, cover designer and illustrator;
    Linda Clavel, illustrator; Juliette Peters, book designer; Karrey Tweten,
    photo researcher

Photo Credits
Corbis/Arne Hodalic, 4; AFP, 6; Earl & Nazima Kowall, 10; Jeremy Horner, 14;
    AFP/Deshakalyan Chowdhury, 16; Sygma/Baldev, 18
Courtesy of The Missionaries of Charity, 8
Getty Images/Hulton Archive, 12, 20; Bangay, cover, 1